Hip-hop dancers

Bobbie Kalman

 Crabtree Publishing Company
www.crabtreebooks.com

Created by Bobbie Kalman

Author and Editor-in-Chief
Bobbie Kalman

Educational consultants
Reagan Miller
Elaine Hurst
Joan King

Editors
Joan King
Reagan Miller
Kathy Middleton

Proofreader
Crystal Sikkens

Design
Bobbie Kalman
Katherine Berti

Photo research
Bobbie Kalman

Production coordinator
Katherine Berti

Prepress technician
Katherine Berti

Photographs by Shutterstock

Library and Archives Canada Cataloguing in Publication

Kalman, Bobbie, 1947-
    Hip-hop dancers / Bobbie Kalman.

(My world)
ISBN 978-0-7787-9431-8 (bound).--ISBN 978-0-7787-9475-2 (pbk.)

    1. Animal behavior--Juvenile literature. I. Title. II. Series: My world (St. Catharines, Ont.)

QL751.5.K335 2010   j591.5   C2009-906066-3

Library of Congress Cataloging-in-Publication Data

Kalman, Bobbie.
 Hip-hop dancers / Bobbie Kalman.
     p. cm. -- (My world)
 ISBN 978-0-7787-9475-2 (pbk. : alk. paper) -- ISBN 978-0-7787-9431-8 (reinforced library binding : alk. paper)
 1. Animal locomotion--Juvenile literature. 2. Dance--Juvenile literature. 3. Stories in rhyme. I. Title. II. Series.

QP310.D35K35 2010
573.7'9--dc22
                                                                            2009041183

Crabtree Publishing Company

Printed in China/122009/CT20091009

www.crabtreebooks.com   1-800-387-7650

Copyright © **2010 CRABTREE PUBLISHING COMPANY**. All rights reserved. No part of this publication may be reproduced, stored in a retrieval system or be transmitted in any form or by any means, electronic, mechanical, photocopying, recording, or otherwise, without the prior written permission of Crabtree Publishing Company. In Canada: We acknowledge the financial support of the Government of Canada through the Book Publishing Industry Development Program (BPIDP) for our publishing activities.

Published in Canada
Crabtree Publishing
616 Welland Ave.
St. Catharines, Ontario
L2M 5V6

Published in the United States
Crabtree Publishing
PMB 59051
350 Fifth Avenue, 59th Floor
New York, New York 10118

Published in the United Kingdom
Crabtree Publishing
Maritime House
Basin Road North, Hove
BN41 1WR

Published in Australia
Crabtree Publishing
386 Mt. Alexander Rd.
Ascot Vale (Melbourne)
VIC 3032

Words to know

bunny

cat

chimpanzee

elephant

sifaka lemur

I am the hip-hop chimpanzee.
I listen to music and sing happily.
When I dance, I sometimes wear my pants!

I dance and dance and dance
every time I have a chance.
I am the hip-hop chimpanzee.

We are the hip-hop cats.
We dance and prance.
We lift our paws high.
We reach for the sky!

We are the hip-hop cats.
When we get tired
and need to relax,
we lie on the floor
and dance on our backs.

Elephants are heavy,
but I am light on my feet.
I love hip-hop dancing.
It is neat!

We are the hip-hop dancing team.
When people see us, they cheer and scream.
We stomp our feet on the ground.
Our friends far away can hear the sound.

I am the hip-hop bunny.
I have big ears that are funny.
To get around, I hip and hop,
but my big ears just flip and flop.

They flip to the left,
and flop to the right.
They flip and flop
while I hip and hop.

My name is Sifaka.
I am the hip-hop lemur.
I am the very best dancer!
Of that, I am sure.

I am a hip-hop master.
No one dances better or faster.
Of that, I am sure.
I am Sifaka, the hip-hop lemur!

Which is the best hip-hop dancer?
Which is the one?
Which is the dancer having the most fun?

Is it flip-flop bunny?

Is it Sifaka, the hip-hop master?

Is it the cat dancer and prancer?

Is it the cool chimpanzee?

Is it the elephant dancers you see?

Notes for adults

Fun, fun, fun!
Hip-hop dancers is a fun book that will delight children. I learned about sifaka lemurs and their dance movements a few years ago. These primates are amazing! They move through the trees by clinging to branches and leaping between tree trunks. They make remarkable leaps of up to 32 feet (10m). On the ground, they hop on two feet and look very much as if they are dancing. They can be seen dancing on the Internet. The easiest way to find them is by searching "Madagascar dancing lemur."

Funny pictures
There are many funny photos of animals, and sometimes it is hard not to anthropomorphize! Photos of chimps are usually funny, as are ones of cats. Children who own cats might want to share stories of how they dance or even take some photos of them dancing. Ask the children to draw pictures of their own hip-hop pets or of the hip-hop dancers shown in this book.

Hip-hop dance
Ask the children to make up some hip-hop movements while they pretend to be cats, chimps, sifakas, rabbits, or elephants. Other students could keep the beat with homemade musical instruments.